Why Adopt ISO Thinking?

The benefits of being ISO9001 certified, compliant or only practicing one element

Robbie Sheerin

Silly Lilly Publishing

Copyright © 2025 Robbie Sheerin

All rights reserved

No part of this book may be reproduced, or stored in a retrieval system, or transmitted in any form or by any means, electronic, mechanical, photocopying, recording, or otherwise, without express written permission of the publisher.

Cover design by: Silly Lilly Publishing
Printed in the United States of America

CONTENTS

Title Page
Copyright
Sources
WHY ADOPT ISO THINKING?
STANDARDIZATION   1
ISO9001;2015 STRUCTURE   10
ISO9001 CERTIFIED, COMPLIANT OR PARTIAL   17
APOPTING ISO THINKING   21
About The Author   37

SOURCES

ISO9001;2015, National Museum of American History, Baltimore Magazine, NISTIR 7158, Mil-Spec various, Berry College, Applied Ergonomics Volume 41 Issue3, ASQ, Lean Six Sigma Pocket Toolbook by Michael l. George, The certified Quality Inspector Handbook.

WHY ADOPT ISO THINKING?

I live in two worlds. By day, I'm a quality manager in the manufacturing industry, and by night I write fiction, mostly science fiction. But all too often our secular and personal lives overlap and mesh together, and this book is the love child of those two worlds—a nonfiction book about quality control. This book is not meant to be a serious, deep read. It's a book for people in manufacturing, from the maintenance guy right up to the president. Its also relatively short book, because people often dont have time to read books, especially work related books. This book however could be use for some short toolbox talks within your own company. The benefits will be transformative.

What makes this book a little different? Firstly, it's not an in-depth book about ISO, but rather the mindset of ISO, the structure it provides, and the chaos it removes. Secondly, maybe people that write books about quality and quality control went to college and may never have actually worked on the shop floor. Coolant under their nails working in those 110-degree shops. If I'm wrong, don't email me, I don't care.

Let me tell you about myself and see if we can make a connection, I will get to the ISO stuff soon. My first experience with manufacturing was at a welding shop, mostly fabrication, fixing plows and boats. In some cases, building boats. I didn't do much in the way of welding, I was more of a helper boy, grabbing coffee, changing grinding disks, holding a clamp in place, and getting shouted at. After about a year, I started working at an aerospace (AS9100) company that made electronic enclosures and many other components for the military, aerospace, medical and commercial industries. Among our customers were Lockheed Martin, Raytheon, BAE, L-3, and Northrop Grumman, to mention a few. I'm sure if you're in the manufacturing industry, these names are familiar to you. As with all the companies I've worked at, machining was also part of their business. I was trained in a process called aluminum dip brazing. What is that, you may ask?

It's a process of fixturing multiple complex machined components together with clamps, springs, swedged taps, or tack welds. A paste or foil is artfully (Please don't think this is an arty farty thing, it's just a technique, but there is an art to it) applied to all the joints. The enclosure or part is warmed up in an oven to around 985 degrees and then slowly lowered into a bath of molten salt, which is around 1,000 degrees. Within less than a minute, the paste or foil has turned to liquid in the way of solder, which now flows through all the joints thanks to capillary action. After around 1–2 minutes, the part is removed and quenched. Once cooled, the part is no longer multiple components but rather one complete unit. This type of process is unique in that tiny parts or huge jointed parts can be brazed together in a way welding never could.

After being heated to 1,000 degrees, aluminum is very soft and can be manipulated and straightened. After being run through an acid line, they are moved to the straightening table to be tapped and bent to meet the customer print. Then the parts are put into another oven at 350 degrees for at least eight hours. After this hardening process (heat-treating), the material can now be machined. Now you can imagine there are lots of instructions and procedures that need to be followed for this type of work. This was my first exposure to AS9100. The need to have paperwork and procedures, and to follow proven instructions and directions.

Temperatures need to be held within a certain tolerance in both ovens. The "salt bath" temperature also needs to be maintained, as well as the correct PH. I had the fun job of "desludging" the salt bath every week. This involved scooping out the sludge from the bottom of the salt bath. Which remember is 1,000 degrees. It actually glows in the dark, it's basically lava. As well as temperatures and PH levels, there are also specific times for parts to be in an oven and in the salt bath. All these aspects need to be controlled and monitored. Any maintenance that needed to be done on the salt bath I did. This included starting up new salt baths, which takes days, swapping out thermocouples and replacing large Inconel electrodes, which are extremely heavy and hot. Part of my job also meant draining acid tanks, then mixing and replacing with new chemicals. Often times I was required to do work outside my department, which included grinding, assembly, shipping and packaging, forklift driving, and even a little engineering design.

After a number of years as a working supervisor, I moved on to two more companies doing the same thing. These were both ISO9001 companies, each certified and with their own version of procedures and work instructions. Each company varies a little, but overall, they need to comply with the standard to which they are certified. So that includes traceability, work instructions, procedures, control of nonconforming products, corrective actions, and effectiveness. MRB, calibration, continuous improvement, training and on and on. With each company, my experience and knowledge grew more and more. I learned to conduct and report TUS (Temperature uniformity test) on ovens and furnaces, calibrating wastewater sensors, machining, and using various measuring devices and systems, soldering and even a little welding.

As I got older, I moved into the quality side of manufacturing, understanding my body was getting beat up day after day and life was too short to continue down that road. But years of working in the real world and "on the shop floor" taught me many lessons and gave me valuable insights that would then help me in the world of quality control and reducing cost.

STANDARDIZATION

The private sector produces most of the products the government requires, such as police cars, government buildings, school buildings, police weapons and uniforms. In an effort to control the quality, they created the MIL-SPEC.

1941-1942 Willys MB

In the late 1930s the army noticed the need to improve on their transportation for messengers, scouts or officers. The use of bikes, horses, or foot was holding them at a disadvantage. Hence, salesman navy commander Charles 'Hary' Payne and civilian consultant for the army Robert Brown, along with Harold Crist and Frank Fenn came up with the idea of the Jeep. A low-profile, high-powered, four-wheel-drive vehicle. Now, of course, the army did not make these, but rather a private car company. In order for car companies to provide products that met the needs of the customer, or in this case the US Army, in 1941 the Mil Specs (Military specifications) were created. This meant that certain materials had to meet a certain standard. Some bolts are made of alloy steel, carbon steel, titanium, or brass. All these types of bolts are used based on the purpose of the product. Nickel bolts are used in harsh environments, like aerospace, chemical processing or marine situations. Brass or copper-zinc are used where electric conductivity is important. Aluminum bolts are used for light-weight applications where corrosion might be a concern. Everything from torque ratings and storage to coating of the material to heat exposure is called out on Mil-Specs.

Now let's say that the Jeep manufacturer decided to use aluminum lug nuts or brass axels, because they were easier or cheaper to manufacture. The result would cause massive failure in the field, resulting in injury or even death. Mil-Specs are used to standardize military objectives in interfacing, design, manufacturing, standard practices, and testing. Within these Military standards, there are dozens of sub-specs. Without this type of standardization, products would constantly fail and never achieve the goal they were intended to reach.

WHY ADOPT ISO THINKING?

Like a frying pan made of plastic or a razor that rusted after exposure to water. Can you imagine?!

In 1979, the British Standard Institution published the BS 5750. These basically were guidelines on developing a quality management system. (QMS) This included key principles pertaining to customer focus (voice of the customer), systematic process approach, documentation, continued improvement, training, and assessment to name a few.

This laid the foundation for the ISO standard. Standardization across industries is paramount to success and, in turn, to society as a whole. Imagine how frustrating it would be baking or cooking with two measuring cups that say "100 Milliliters," yet one actually only holds 75 milliliters and the other 100 milliliters. Or a box of one-inch nails that also contained 3/4-inch nails.

1904 The Great Baltimore fire.

One of the biggest failures in history due to the lack of standardization was in 1904, during the great Baltimore fire. With 1,231 firefighters, 57 fire engines, nine trucks, two hose companies, one fire boat and one police boat, the fire still raged on for thirty plus hours. 1,526 buildings were destroyed. A total of 2,500 businesses were lost. More than 30,000 people were left unemployed, and a staggering $150 million in damages, which in today's money is into the billions. Incredibly, only one person died. Why was the destruction and cost so large? Threads!! Firefighters could not get enough water because of the variety of threads on the hydrants and the hoses.

It was discovered later by the National Bureau of Standards that there were over 600 sizes and variations in fire hose couplings across the US. The following year, a standard-sized coupling and fire hydrant were established.

In 1987, ISO (International Organization of Standardization) published the first ISO9001 Standard. The ISO9001 standard can seem vague and is often open to interpretation, in that it does not tell you step by step how to run a company or how to manufacture products. But rather, it provides guidelines and structure. Having a standardized system means multiple companies around the world do things basically the same way. This gives customers a window into the company, allowing them to build confidence that the supplier has the needed goals and values to produce their product. Being ISO (on some level) would mean they meet the standard and have a level of competence to carry out work for them. Its like going to Starbucks, you know the coffee is basically the same in Boston and in LA. Why? Because their product and services are standard throughout the company. The same is true of ISO companies. That status means they have all the structure, mechanisms and elements in place to provide a quality product or service.

What does standardization look like in the real-world?

Maybe its the way HR files paperwork. All the people involved in this process, would do it the same way according to their procedure. Remember, "say as you do, do as you say." This would mean no one should be going rogue.

If some raw material is to be deburred BEFORE it is put into a machine, then everyone needs to do that, not just one person. You should not have another operator deciding it can be done afterwards or by someone else in a different department. If steps are skipped or done in the wrong order problems WILL plague a process and escapes WILL happen.

There may be times when some of the ISO9001 standard simply does not apply to a company.

8.3 of the standard provides guidance for design. Some companies do not provide any design services, so this would not apply to them.

7.1.5.2 of the standard provides guidance for calibration. Again, some companies do not have equipment that would need calibrated.

Because of the various companies and products out there in the world, ISO has published other standards such as;

ISO9001;2015 Quality management
ISO14000 Environment management
ISO45001 Health and safety
ISO50001 Energy management

ISO22000 Food Safety

ISO/IEC 27001 IT security

AS9100 Quality management system for aerospace (Not published by ISO, but incorporates all of ISO9001, and is often used instead of ISO9001)

ISO9001 Quality Management System-Requirements is what I am most familiar with, so this is what this book will refer to, but the ideas and logic of this book should be adopted with any ISO or AS9100 standard. The value of these guidelines and structure can be of great importance to any company or employee wishing to be successful.

Lean ideology is another aspect of manufacturing which often goes hand in hand with ISO. Some of the examples in this book are lean thinking. Lean is another powerful tool that can be used in part or in full in reducing or eliminating waste and improving efficiency. There are seven types of waste that have been identified in companies, these are;

1. Overproduction
2. Waiting
3. Unnecessary transportation of products or materials

4. Overprocessing
5. Inventory
6. Unnecessary employee movement
7. Production of defective parts.

All these are money eaters. The thought behind the lean process is "doing more with less." By removing clutter and unused equipment or tools for example from a work station, an area can start to become streamlined. Think about this for a moment; How much time is wasted looking for something amongst a mess? Trying to find a tool in a messy toolbox, or trying to find a file in a system full of redundant paperwork. Add all those minutes up in a week, month or year. Figure out out much it costs. Now multiple that by the amount of employees there are. It's a lot of money!!!

ISO9001;2015 STRUCTURE

I won't bore you with all the ins and outs of the 29-page ISO9001;2015. This isn't a book about learning ISO, it's about changing your mindset of structure and quality, and the benefits of it within your own company or workplace. All elements of the standard are important and need to be met to attain ISO9001 certification. However, some that read this book may choose not to, or are unable to pay for or allocate time and resources to become certified. Therefore, I will review, based on my humble experience of getting dirty on the shop floor to working behind a computer what I feel is vital for producing quality products and acquiring customer satisfaction, if you chose to simply adopt ISO thinking. A little more on that later.

Being both, compliant or certified have benefits, and obviously one is more robust than the other. Maybe by reading this book, you will take the steps to become compliant or maybe advance from compliant to certified. Either way you will benefit by changing your mindset and structure, even just applying one element of ISO

The elements of ISO9001 are;
- Leadership
- Planning
- Support
- Operation
- Performance evaluation
- Improvement

Even just looking at these six areas, you can see structure and flow.

Leadership. 5.0 It starts at the top: CEO's, CFO's, managers, supervisors. Leaders need to be the driving force behind any changes in a company, and with that also means taking responsibility for the failures as well as the improvements. There must be no doubt or negativity from a leader towards a good quality management system. They must be on-board with change and growth, even if at first it costs them time, money and resources. Companies will make more money in the long run. Leaders must see the bigger picture. By utilizing ISO, the picture or health of their company will become clearer.

Planning. 6.0 Like anything we do, planning is vital for success. Did you ever run out of gas? Ever forget something for your vacation because you didn't pack the night before a flight? Ever not get enough paint or bags of mulch because you didn't calculate first? It's inevitable that if we don't have the proper foresight, something will be overlooked or forgotten.

Alexander Graham Bell once said, "Preparation is the key to success." Not planning within a company or business leads to headaches, failures, scrap and cost. In some cases, it can even lead to loss of customers or contracts. In recent years, ISO and quality control have focused more on risk-based thinking. This means before anything happens, goals, risks, opportunities, and objectives are reviewed, and what procedures and safety mechanisms (To avoid unwanted results such as scrap, defects, and late deliveries.) will be utilized.

Support: 7.0 No company can build anything without resources. This includes people, infrastructure, and environment. And then how are resources supported to achieve our goals and objectives? Is the equipment up to date, is it maintained (In most cases calibrated), and is it safe? How are concerns about resources communicated, recorded, and tracked? Are employees competent and aware? If not, what support do they have from upper management? Is everything documented? What is the difference between a document and a record? I heard this expression once, and it's good to keep in mind. "Documents say do, records say done."

E.g. 1. A procedure (Document) says that the company will calibrate their gages once per year. A calibration cert (Record) shows that it was calibrated.

E.g. 2. A procedure (Document) says that the company will perform a first-piece inspection before every production run. An inspection report (Record) is filled out.

Operation: 8.0 This is where all the planning and resources are put into action. Customer requirements or services must be met. Proper safeguards and SOP's are used to maintain customer requirements. How are changes to the customer requirements handled this late in the game? How are outside sources handled? At times outside vendors are used, but they themselves may not be ISO certified. Who is responsible for handling certified/uncertified vendors and any defects or issues that occur? How are nonconformances being investigated, resolved and documented?

Performance evaluation: 9.0 This is where data is vital to understanding the health of a project or company. I have heard many people say, "Numbers and data don't matter as long as we are making good parts, who cares." On the face of it, it's true. At the end of the day, good-quality products are what's most important. However, what did it take to get those quality products? What did the journey look like?

It's like a king's messenger delivering a message to an army in a foreign land. Sure, he got there and delivered the message. But was he on-time? Did any soldiers perish because of his lateness? How many people tried to kill him on his journey? How many times did he almost starve to death? How many rivers did he have to swim across? How many injuries or infections did he have to overcome?

"I have a message, but I almost died getting it here."

Data gathering throughout the process will show what obstacles were faced and how much time and effort was expended. Why did a process take so long, or why did it fail? Why did the product have to be made and reworked multiple times? (This is known as the hidden factory, a money pit that often goes unnoticed.) Why were the parts late? All these questions, if reviewed and resolved, can produce a quality product at a cheaper price in a faster time the next time around. And that means more profits, which should lead to better equipment, raises (hopefully), lunch for employees, fewer headaches and more contracts. And this is where the final step comes in. Improvement.

Improvement: 10.0 Now that we have a detailed picture of the messenger's journey (Manufacturing or service), we can begin to make changes so he won't almost die the next time. We can buy a second machine, cross-train employees, require that we buy better raw materials, increase inspections, retrain employees, reduce movement of parts from one workstation to another, invest in better equipment, and change a process. This information will allow you to put money or resources in the most cost-effective areas. (E.g. Do you really need a new machine, or do you simply need to train the operator better?) All this is done through a study of not only data but failures. E.g. nonconformities.

Two important words often used in companies are "continuous improvement." Every company should strive for this. It's another key to success and shows ISO thinking. And the fact that it's continuous means it should never end. Unfortunately, the words "we have always made it this way" or "Ship it, it will be fine" are also very common in the manufacturing world. This type of thinking and speech is toxic in a company. I approached a CEO once and informed him that we needed to address a couple of small things before an audit. He told me "He didn't care." At another company, an engineer told me after a concern over a Rev on a drawing, "So what, so we get a minor finding, big deal." I told him if you get enough minor findings they become major findings. This type of talk and thinking from senior people takes the wind out of any good that is trying to be done, and immediately deflates the progress a company is trying to make. Improving must come from the top, and their words have huge impact for good and bad. Taking the steps of being certified to ISO9001, being compliant or practicing a portion of ISO9001 is continuous improvement. For those that do this, you should be commended. It shows you care about your company, product and reputation. And when an auditor or customer comes knocking, you will be able to welcome them with confidence.

ISO9001 CERTIFIED, COMPLIANT OR PARTIAL

To me, there are three options for companies who want to improve in quality, reduce cost and attain customer satisfaction. Obviously, being ISO9001 *certified* (Accredited by an external third party) is the top option, with the highest cost but also the most benefits. This status takes the most resources to implement and maintain. And with that comes higher quality and the most opportunities for increased work and contracts. The next option is being *compliant* (Self-declared status with no external certification). This is an interesting one, in that it takes all the same resources as certification, however, it does not have the same cost in that you will not need to pay the accreditor every year for a certification. In this scenario, it is possible for some companies to still use you without an ISO certification, but be warned if you claim you are compliant, be ready to prove that, during a customer audit. The third option, is to simply implement *partial* elements of ISO. Often times, this will not get you top tier work. But again, this is another interesting option. Why?

Some companies are small, with only a few employees or even a small product line. But choosing to implement internal audits, for example, can greatly reduce cost and scrap. These can also be conducted in-house, further reducing cost and increasing customer satisfaction and quality. We will get into this in the next chapter.

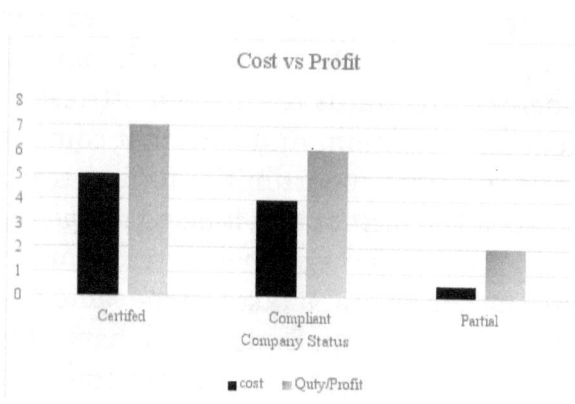

This chart above is not accurate and is not to be taken as actual data. But I want to show that all options produce positive results. Some may argue that simply reducing scrap or overwork on one single job or product can increase profits. This is true. Take a look at the following example of introducing the investigation of nonconformities.

Let's say the customer wants a brass connector. But every time these are produced, there is a small burr around the ID. It has always been removed by hand as a secondary operation in the finishing department. One day the customer complains that the burr is not completely removed or that there are scratches where the burr was removed. A CAR (Corrective Action Report) is created and investigated. During the investigation, it is discovered that the operator does not have adequate hand tools for this job. It also takes the operator 4 hours to rework 500 parts by hand. After reviewing the process or technique used and cost analysis, it is discovered that by adding a 5-second pass of the part in the machine, the burr can be removed. Now you have removed the rework op and gone from 4 hours to 41 minutes (extra machine time). That's a 17% saving, or an increase depending on how you look at it. And that's on one job that you may produce multiple times in a year.

Having the resources to segregate parts, stop production, conduct root cause analysis, and fix the problem is a major win for a company. It should never be "Don't stop the machine" or "keep production running." Obviously, we want to avoid having late shipments, at times, this is unavoidable. But I always say it's better to be late and provide quality parts, than be on time and provide inadequate parts. If a problem or nonconformance is found, production should stop until it has been resolved along with <u>the help of QC</u>. (Often times, it is the operators, programmers and engineers that resolve manufacturing issues.) However, it is QC that needs to document all the details and corrective actions and to deal with the customer. In order to do that, they need to be fully involved in the matter on the floor. As the voice of the company as to quality concerns, the quality manager must have a complete picture of the cause and corrections. This is of vital importance and cannot be stated enough.) In my experience, if this is not done at the first sign of an issue, the issue will repeat, repeat, repeat. And that my friends is insanity, and customers don't like insane companies. The down time to resolve a problem will absolutely be worth it in the long run. Continuous improvement will always pay off.

APOPTING ISO THINKING

As an operator, quality inspector and finally a quality manager at multiple companies over the years, I have discovered some of the most important elements of the ISO standard. These are only my experiences and opinions. Others may have their own thoughts and ideas on this matter. Of course, the whole ISO9001 standard should be used as they all flow and connect to each other. But again, there are some that are either not convinced of this investment or are just too small to invest the time, money and resources. This is why I wrote this book to convince owners, at a minimum, of the wisdom of adopting ISO thinking. This book is also for all employees to see the value in ISO thinking and procedures. Unfortunately, ISO and the thinking behind it can be foreign to operators and owners with a frustrated quality team in the middle.

Internal audits. Internal audits are performed in order to ensure customer, industry, statutory, the standard and regulatory requirements are being followed. To determine the effectiveness of the work being done, and if there are any areas for improvement as to reducing scrap and improving quality.

There is a lot to an audit, but basically, the auditor will gather information as to the department or area they wish to audit. This would involve reviewing work instructions and procedures and following the operator around as they carry out their responsibilities. Once they have familiarized themselves with the area and work, they will interview the employee, asking such questions as, what are your responsibilities? What training did you get? How do you know what to do? ect. The questions are generally the same in audits, but some answers can lead to other questions. Evidence needs to be provided to back up the employee's answers. After the interview, the auditor will take all his/her information, evidence and notes and review it to see if it satisfies the standard. (In cases where the company is NOT certified or compliant, the audit can be reviewed against any work instructions or reviewed at the management level for any issues. But in most cases, there are some written instructions the employee should be following.)

After the audit is complete a report is compiled of what, if any, improvements can be made. If the company is ISO certified, then findings need to be reported and corrective actions need to be opened, investigated and closed without undue delay. Some who are not ISO certified may choose to do this anyway. It would be wise. Again, keeping in mind "continuous improvement." This report is provided to and discussed with management. But again, not to point fingers but to improve the system.

People are often afraid of internal audits. They roll their eyes, run to the nearest closet, sweat bullets—you've seen it, maybe you've reacted that way, but they should be viewed as a good thing. Remember we are auditing the system, not the people. The internal auditor and the operator are a team, not enemies. It's a way to grow, and if carried out correctly, people and a company can improve.

Fix the holes before you go to sea

View a company like a boat that has a bunch of holes

in it. Wouldn't you want to fix them all before you go to sea? Conducting internal audits will reveal all the holes in your company and keep you afloat as you move forward. They will also allow you to fix issues before an external audit. And expect to find holes and issues. We are all creatures of habit, and typically these bad habits creep back in. View internal audits as a company reset. A couple of things to note, internal auditors do not need to be officially trained, however they do need to be unbiased in the areas they audit and they need to be impartial.

Nonconformity and corrective actions. I've touched on this a few times but its important. In an effort to continue to improve, nonconformities need to be handled effectively. Its not enough to say, we fixed the parts and moved on. But we need to dig down deeper to find out the whys. Some of you may have used the hated 5whys. Although on the face of it, you may feel like you're talking to a five-year-old, the 5why process is very powerful. But even if you don't deploy this tool, its important to keep asking the questions.

Why did the spoon have a sharp edge? Because the machine didn't clean the edge correctly. **Why?** Because the tool had become dull. **Why?** Because we kept using it beyond its tool life. **Why?** Because no one check the condition of the tool. **Why?** Because it wasn't on the checklist.

Sure, the reason for the nonconforming spoon is because of the sharp edge. But when you go a little further and keep asking like a five-year-old, you get to the underling cause. *The root* cause was because tool inspection was not on the check list. *Corrective action-* Add tool inspection to the checklist. Don't just stop at the first answer, go further, dig deeper, find the roots and yank them out. This will pay off, resulting in future success machining the spoons, but you will also find other opportunities where tool inspections should be added to your process. Remember cutting down a bush doesn't stop it from growing back, removing the roots does.

With many aspects of ISO, recording everything is very important. This is the case with nonconformities and corrective actions. These need to be documented. Why? If you are ISO certified, you need to show that you can improve quality and handle nonconformance's effectively and avoid dissatisfaction from customers through repeated escapes, it also helps identify deficiencies within the process or company. If you simply just want to follow this one element of ISO, the benefits are the same, but also documentation can be referred back to, to research previous issues and how they were fixed. If defects result again, you will have history of the issue and what you implemented to fix them. Documentation can also help you narrow down where the failures are in your organization, not just processes. E.g. infrastructure, equipment, people or outside services.

At times a trend may appear in your collection of CAR's, where it is clear that more training is needed, or a position needs to be created, or new knowledge needs to be acquired. Handling nonconformance's and corrective actions again is like patching the holes in a boat, it will keep you alive when you're at sea. Its not enough to remove the water over and over, you must patch the holes. Or even take it a step further, why are there holes in the boat in the first place? The holes aren't the real issue, maybe it's the nails on the trailer that you carry your boat on, but I digress. But a good example of digging deeper.

Process approach. The word 'process' or a variation of it is mentioned 114 times in the ISO9001 standard. A process is a journey to achieve a goal. A procedure or work instruction are the steps within that journey or process. With each image below, the details get greater. Again, there is more to this and different variation, this is only to give you an idea of what the process approach looks like. This type of ISO thinking creates structure and removes the confusion.

WHY ADOPT ISO THINKING?

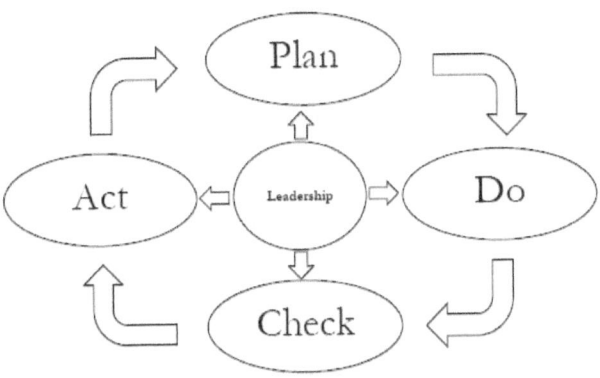

PDCA Process

Key people that should be involved in this are executive leaders, quality assurance, supervisors and engineers. Sometimes buyers or purchasing is involved too. The purpose of including these people is that every department has input and all have a part to play in the process. One departments problem should be the other departments problem too because they are all interconnected. At times this can actually lead to a department taking on another responsibility that works better for the whole process. Why is the PDCA process in a circle and not a flow chart? You guessed it, 'continuous improvement.' You keep going around and around until you have flushed out all the defects. Its like a dirty rug, cleaning it once never gets all the dirt out. But cleaning it over and over weeds out all the grime. You should strive to be the best you can be and the process approach is the best way to do this.

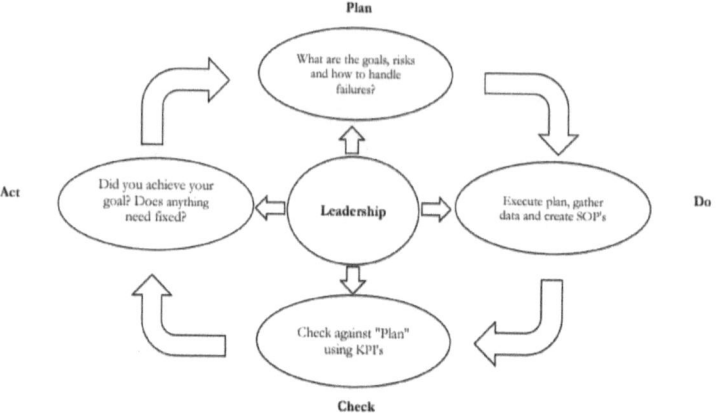

In the above example, we see what information was needed for each procedure or step. Who will do what? Who will study the SOP and adjust them if we need to? When will we start the project? Who is ordering material or supplies? Ect.

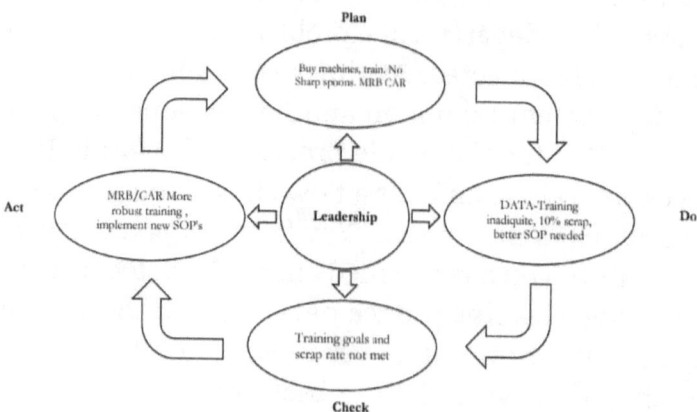

The above example is a little different and can run

alongside the previous one. What issues could happen? Hard material could mean excessive tool wear-Parts could be assembled backwards-Lead times on raw materials or services could be long. **How can we handle these issues proactively? What can we do to limit these issues before we start?** Ect.

Internal audits, handling nonconformities and **process control** can all improve customer satisfaction, quality and reduce cost. One or all of these can be adopted into your company. Adopted in one department or multiple, the effects can be transformative and potent.

Some Final Thoughts and Suggestions

I have found many practices and philosophies that are effective in continuous improvement. One of these is a powerful tool that can be adopted into our process: a "poka-yoke" (A Japanese expression that means 'Mistake-proofing'. In the western world, we call it idiot proofing. A little more offensive than the Japanese) Have you ever had assembly issues? Components left out of an assembly or inserted backwards? We have all seen it; the row of plastic bins or boxes, each containing the components for an assembly. The operator removes each component(s) and inserts it into a casing. It becomes monotonous, and they can be distracted at various steps in the procedure, returning and forgetting what has been assembled and what has not. Something

I have found that works effectively is the example below.

1. Fill entire tray matching picture with parts. (Picture in the bottom of each compartment)

2. Assemble 1a,b,c,d,e,f,g then 1a,b,c,d,e,f,g then 3a,b,c,d,e,f,g then 4a,b,c,d,e,f,g. Only remove ONE component at a time and assemble.

3. Do not move on to next number until previous row is complete

4. Do not remove final assemblies until all four assemblies are complete

5. Return to step 1

WHY ADOPT ISO THINKING?

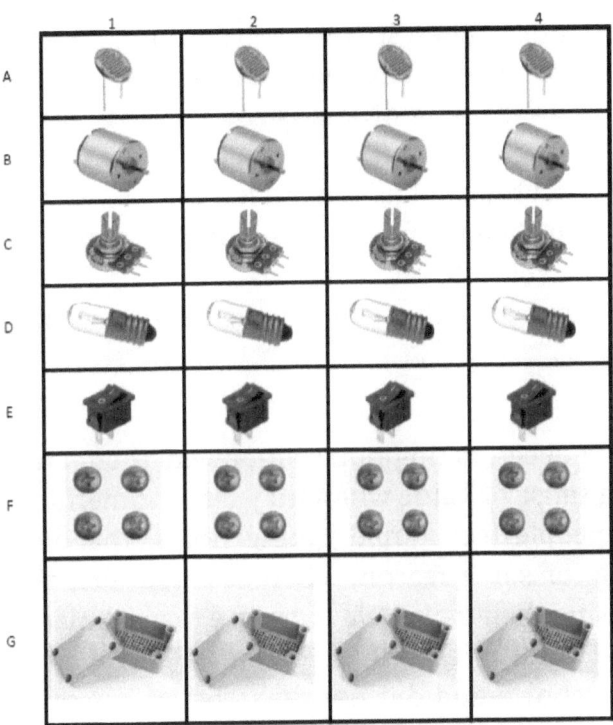

What I found to be effective in this example is the visual aspect of the tray. When the tray is full, you know you have all the components for the assembly—no more, no less. You also visually see the order of assembly. And another huge advantage here is that if at any point you leave the station or are distracted, you can return and see exactly where you left off. Try it, do a little study, and see if this or a variation of it works within your company.

Another technique I have found to be very helpful-

Taking notes. When it comes to training new people, most people hate it. But one of the biggest reasons why people hate training others is the fact that they don't listen or retain the information. Every job I have ever worked at, I took notes. When I left one company, I had a one-inch notepad full of notes and drawings. I'm not a nerd, I just like to know how to do stuff. No one wants to have to ask someone five times how to do the same thing.

For employees, taking notes empowers them and gives them a sense of value when they learn something new. Some people feel stupid taking notes, that they are lacking for some reason, when in actual fact they are increasing their value. We therefore made it mandatory to take notes within that company. This way, people had no choice and did not feel singled out as a 'note taker.' It works wonders, and you will be amazed at how much time this will save later and how more competent your employees will become. A warning though, it's vital that the trainer slow down and allow people to take the notes in their own way and in a format they can understand and recall. And with this said, it's never one and done; remember, there still may be follow up questions later, but hopefully way less.

Whether you are certified, compliant or practicing one element, adopting ISO thinking means shifting our mind and thinking clearly and systematically. Slow down and don't just think about shipments and profits, those increases and benefits will come later. Do a little work at the start, and the benefits will reveal themselves like a hidden treasure. Take the time to fix the nails on the boat trailer, you will be glad you did when you're at sea. Be proactive, not reactive!!! Fix the root cause, there's no point changing a moldy rug if you haven't fixed a leaky roof first. Why not get copies of this book for your whole company and start improving today!!!

If you have found this book helpfull please share with your colleagues and also take a moment to write a review on amazon. THANK YOU!!

WHY ADOPT ISO THINKING?

ABOUT THE AUTHOR

Robbie Sheerin

Robbie Sheerin was born in Scotland but has lived in the US for more than twenty years. He works as a quality manager in the manufacturing industry, and lives in the Boston area with his wife. Robbie has multiple scifi books to his name, as well as a monthly blog of short stories. This is his first nonfiction work.
www.Robbiesheerinwriter.com

www.ingramcontent.com/pod-product-compliance
Lightning Source LLC
Chambersburg PA
CBHW031552210526
45464CB00003B/1276